This book is given to

on

the
little
spider

the little spider

a story about giving written by

SIGMUND BROUWER

with original song by

CINDY MORGAN

illustrated by

SUSAN KATHLEEN HARTUNG

TYNDALE HOUSE PUBLISHERS, INC.
WHEATON, ILLINOIS

Visit Tyndale's exciting Web site at www.tyndale.com

Designed by Julie Chen

Library of Congress Cataloging-in-Publication Data

Brouwer, Sigmund, date.
    The little spider / Sigmund Brouwer.
      p. cm.
    Summary: A group of animals vows to protect the Holy Family, but when Herod's soldiers close in it is the tiny
spider whose gift hides the cave in which the Child sleeps.
    ISBN 0-8423-3918-3 (alk. paper)
    1. Jesus Christ—Nativity—Legends. [1. Jesus Christ—Nativity—Legends. 2. Spiders—Folklore. 3. Animals—Folklore.
4. Folklore.] I. Title.

PZ8.1.B796 Li 2001
398.24′52544—dc21
[E]   2001027217

Printed in Korea

07 06 05 04 03 02 01
7   6   5   4   3   2   1

For Olivia,

We love you.

 ONG AGO, ON A WINTER
NIGHT IN A VILLAGE
OUTSIDE THE HILLS OF
Jerusalem

Mouse ran to the doorway
of the stable.

"Wake up! Wake up!" Mouse shouted.

In the stable, Cat slept against the warmth of Dog,
both of them half covered with straw. Dog snored softly,
occasionally shaking his head when straw tickled his
nostrils. Nearby, Donkey slept too.

"Wake up! Wake up!" Mouse shouted again.

At Mouse's voice, Cat lifted her head. She had very sharp

ears. Dog twitched in his sleep, but Donkey was lost in dreams of carrots and shade on a hot day and buckets of cold, clean water.

Mouse saw that Cat was awake. Instead of running directly across the stable, which would take him within leaping distance of Cat, Mouse scurried along the walls until he reached Donkey's feet.

"Wake up! Wake up!" Mouse shouted.

But to a donkey deep in sleep, a mouse's shout is not very loud. So Donkey did not even open one tired eye.

Mouse ran up Donkey's front leg and onto Donkey's back.

"Wake up! Wake up!" Mouse shouted.

But Donkey was old. He did not wake easily.

Mouse climbed up Donkey's mane and perched between Donkey's ears.

"Wake up! Wake up!" Mouse shouted.

Still Donkey did not wake. Mouse twisted one of Donkey's ears and shouted into it. "Wake up!"

Donkey blinked his eyes open.

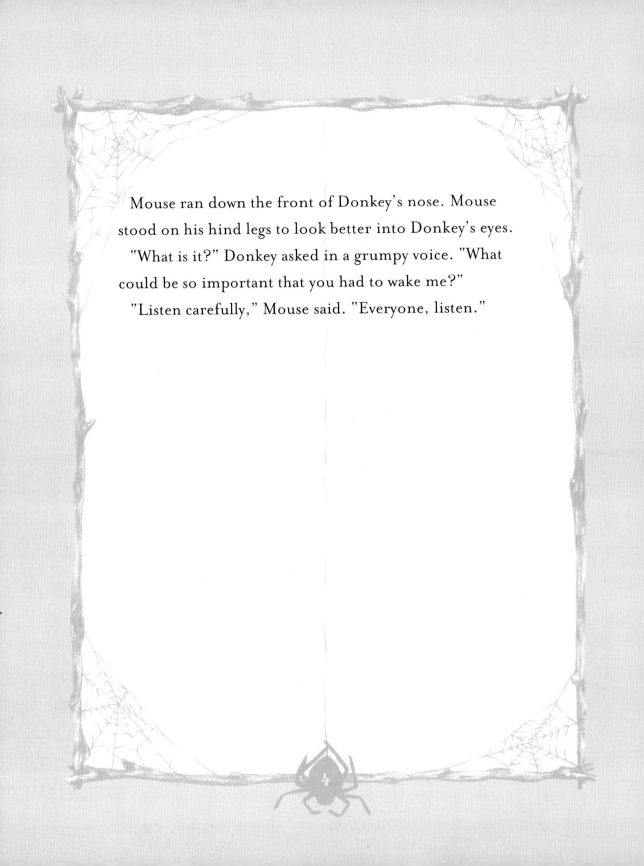

Mouse ran down the front of Donkey's nose. Mouse stood on his hind legs to look better into Donkey's eyes.

"What is it?" Donkey asked in a grumpy voice. "What could be so important that you had to wake me?"

"Listen carefully," Mouse said. "Everyone, listen."

two

AN AND WOMAN ARE LEAVING," MOUSE TOLD DONKEY. MOUSE TURNED AND LOOKED DOWN ON DOG AND CAT. "TONIGHT."

By now, Dog was awake too. Dog slowly rose to his feet as Cat arched her back and stretched. They stood in the straw at Donkey's feet and looked upward at Mouse.

"Tonight?" Cat asked. She paused to lick her forearm and rub it across her whiskers. "No one travels at night. The hills are too dangerous. Filled with bandits."

"You know I live in their home across from the stable,"

Mouse said. Mouse tried to keep his voice strong. It made him nervous to watch Cat clean her whiskers. "I heard Man tell Woman they must go. Tonight. Even now, they are packing all they can carry."

Donkey sighed. "Not all *they* can carry. All *I* can carry."

Cat stared at Mouse thoughtfully and continued to clean her whiskers.

"Why?" Dog asked Mouse. "Did you find out why they would do such a foolish thing?"

Mouse nodded. "The Man told the Woman he was warned in a dream. By an angel."

"Angel?" Donkey asked, suddenly much more awake.

Of them all, Donkey was the only one who had seen angels. It had happened the night that the Child was born, when Man and Woman had been forced to share another stable with Donkey. Many times Dog and Cat and Mouse had asked Donkey to tell the story of that starry night, when the sky was filled with angels who sang to the world about the Child. And Donkey had gladly told them again and again how the angels

had promised the Child would bring peace to all the world.

"It was an angel," Mouse repeated. "In this dream, the angel told Man to leave quickly, because King Herod is going to search for the Child to kill him."

"Kill the Child!" Donkey said. "But why?"

"King Herod is afraid the Child will take over Israel and become the greatest king of all," Mouse said, proudly sharing his important news. "Herod has sent soldiers. They have their orders. The Child must not live."

"No!" Donkey said, stamping his feet in fear. "We can't let that happen! I will take them far away."

"I will go with you," Mouse said, shaking a fist as if he actually stood defiant before the terrible King Herod. "No matter how far the journey. I will never leave the Child."

"Nor shall I leave the Child," Cat said. Cat licked a front paw and studied it to make sure it was completely clean. "Surely along the journey I will find a way to help the Child."

"I will guard them," Dog announced. Dog puffed his chest. "I will make sure no harm comes to the Child."

"Please let me come too," said a small, small voice, so small it was almost a whisper.

three

ALL OF THEM TURNED TO THE SMALL, SMALL VOICE. IT CAME FROM THE DARKNESS OF AN UPPER CORNER.

"You?" Mouse asked. "You?"

Mouse laughed. "I have keen ears. I will listen for danger and give warning as we travel. How can you possibly help the Child?"

Cat laughed. "My paws are quick, and my claws are sharp. I can protect the Child as we travel. What can you possibly give to the Child?"

Dog laughed. "I have strong bones and big teeth. I too

can protect the Child as we travel. Stay in the stable, Little Spider. The king's soldiers will crush you with one step and not even know you were there."

"Yes, let us bigger animals protect the Child," Mouse said with pride. "A little spider like you will only get in the way."

"All the times Donkey has told you about the night of angels, I too have listened from up here. I too know the Child is special." Little Spider moved closer. "Whatever I can do or give to help the Child, I will."

Mouse and Cat and Dog laughed one more time at Little Spider. Mouse ran down Donkey's leg and jumped on Dog's back, which was still a safe distance from Cat. Then Mouse and Cat and Dog ignored Little Spider. They began to plan all the great deeds they would do to protect the Child.

Donkey merely waited to carry the load that would be placed upon him.

And without another word to Mouse or Cat or Dog or Donkey, Little Spider left his safe home in the high

corner of the stable. It was a great distance down the wall and across the floor and up Donkey's front leg to reach Donkey's mane, but Little Spider did not complain. Even if Little Spider had no keen ears, or quick paws and sharp claws, or strong bones and big teeth to help protect the Child, Little Spider wanted to stay with the Child.

four

OON AFTER, MAN AND WOMAN APPEARED IN THE STABLE. DONKEY STOOD PATIENTLY AS THEY PLACED BUNDLES OF ALL THAT THEY OWNED UPON HIS BACK.

In Woman's arms was the Child, asleep. All of the animals knew the Child was special.

On this night, Donkey did not pull against the rope, as he usually did. On this night, Donkey gladly followed as Man led him out of the stable.

Dog and Cat followed behind. Little Spider stayed in Donkey's mane.

Mouse stopped at the edge of the straw and did not go out of the stable into the night.

Dog and Cat ran back.

"What is it?" Dog asked Mouse. "I thought you wanted to remain with the Child, no matter how far we journeyed."

"Why have you stopped?" Cat asked Mouse. "We must hurry and follow."

A large, round moon threw beautiful silver light onto the ground at the edge of the stable.

Mouse's whiskers twitched as he looked into the great sky and at the dark shadows cast by the moon. "I love the Child. You know that. But I have to admit I am only a mouse. My legs are short and my body is tiny. The world out there is so large that I know there is nothing I can do to help the Child. Perhaps it would be best if I remained here."

"If that is what you choose," Cat said to Mouse. "But I am going with the Child. Nothing will force me to leave. My paws are quick and my claws are sharp. I can protect the Child as we travel."

"If that is what you choose," Dog said to Mouse. "But I am going with the Child. I have strong bones and big teeth. I will protect the Child no matter what happens."

From the mane of Donkey, Little Spider called back to Mouse. "Come with us," Little Spider said. Even if Little Spider had no keen ears, or quick paws and sharp claws, or strong bones and big teeth to help protect the Child, Little Spider wanted to stay with the Child.

But Mouse had already turned back into the stable to hide in the straw where it would be safe and warm.

five

O IT WAS THAT MAN
AND WOMAN AND THE
CHILD LEFT BEHIND
THEIR HOME IN BETH-
LEHEM AND TRAVELED
INTO THE COLD OF A CLEAR WINTER NIGHT.

The stars filled the black velvet above them, and the light
of that large, silver moon cast dark shadows. The light
of the moon allowed Donkey to travel easily on the path
among the hills.

Yet Donkey worried greatly. The very light that showed
Donkey the path was the very light that would let Herod's
soldiers travel quickly too as they chased the family.

Donkey walked as fast as he could.

Sometimes Dog would run back and watch the path to see if Herod's soldiers were close.

Another hour passed as they traveled long, difficult miles on that path among the steep hills, until there came a point when they had to stop.

As they rested, Cat sniffed the air.

"This is wonderful," Cat said to Dog. "Can you smell all the different and exciting smells? I never knew all of this world existed beyond the stable!"

"Stay close by," Dog answered. "Remember, we are here to protect the Child."

Cat's ears perked up at strange, interesting little sounds in the shadows beyond the path. "I love the Child. You know that. But I have to admit I am only a cat. And the Child has you and Donkey to help. What can a cat do that you can't do much better? Perhaps it would be best if I remained here."

"If that is what you choose," Dog said to Cat. "But I am going with the Child. I have strong bones and big teeth. I will protect the Child no matter what happens."

From the mane of Donkey, Little Spider called back to Cat. "Come with us." Even if Little Spider had no keen ears, or quick paws and sharp claws, or strong bones and big teeth to help protect the Child, Little Spider wanted to stay with the Child.

But Cat had already scampered into the shadows beyond the path to chase after all the exciting new smells and sounds in the hills.

six

GAIN THE FAMILY
BEGAN TO TRAVEL INTO
THE COLD OF A CLEAR
WINTER NIGHT. ONLY
DOG FOLLOWED DONKEY
NOW. LITTLE SPIDER, TOO, REMAINED
WITH DONKEY.

Again they traveled long, difficult miles on that path
among the steep hills, until again there came a point
when they had to stop. Man found a cave and brought
all of them inside.

Donkey and Dog and Little Spider listened as Man
explained to Woman. They would sleep the remaining

few hours until the sun rose. They would continue then, fleeing Bethlehem for Egypt, where they would be safe from Herod. But only if they survived the night.

As Man and Woman and the Child slept, the soldiers marched closer and closer.

"I am getting cold," Dog whispered to Donkey. "I want to walk and run to keep warm. I will go look for the soldiers. I have strong bones and big teeth. When I find them, I can protect the Child."

"Yes," Donkey said. "Otherwise, what will we do? Man and Woman and the Child are too tired. The soldiers will catch up to them if they continue. The soldiers will catch up to them if we wait here. And the soldiers will not let the Child live."

"I will go meet the soldiers," Dog said. "I will fight them before they reach the cave."

So Dog ran out of the cave. He followed the path back toward Bethlehem, and within a few miles, Dog saw Herod's soldiers.

As Dog neared the soldiers, the silver light of the moon

clearly showed there were many. All armed with swords and spears. All well protected by shields.

Dog stopped and hid in the shadows beneath a bush. Dog spoke quietly, as if Donkey might be able to hear and understand. "I love the Child. You know that. But I have to admit I am only a dog. And there are many soldiers. Who was I to think I could protect the Child from Herod? Perhaps it would be best if I remained here until they passed by."

So Dog hid quietly and did not return to protect the Child.

And the soldiers moved closer and closer to the cave ahead where the Child slept with Donkey and Little Spider nearby. Even if Little Spider had no keen ears, or quick paws and sharp claws, or strong bones and big teeth to help protect the Child, Little Spider wanted to stay with the Child.

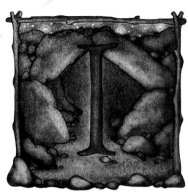

seven

N THE CAVE, MAN
AND WOMAN AND
THE CHILD SLEPT.

As did Donkey, who once again
dreamed of carrots and shade on
a hot day and buckets of clean, cold water.

Little Spider was awake.

Little Spider watched the Child from Donkey's back.
Little Spider was drawn to the Child, as surely as if God's
love had been shining like a warm and wonderful light out
of the darkness.

Little Spider felt great joy to be in the presence of the
Child.

But Little Spider was also sad.

The Child shivered as he slept in the cold of the cave.

Little Spider wished badly that he could keep the Child warm.

"I am only a little spider," Little Spider whispered, "and I do not have much to give. But I will do and give what I can."

Little Spider began to spin a web across the entrance of the cave, hoping to make a curtain to keep out the cold.

What Little Spider didn't know was that outside the cave, Herod's soldiers marched closer and closer along the path beneath the silver light of the moon. Closer and closer to the cave that held Man and Woman and the Child.

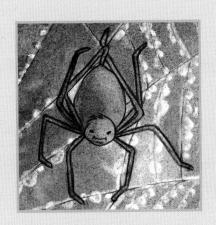

eight

T WAS SO COLD OUTSIDE THE CAVE THAT FROST BEGAN TO COLLECT ON THE GROUND. AS LITTLE SPIDER SPUN HIS WEB, SO TOO DID FROST BEGIN TO COVER THE STRANDS ACROSS THE ENTRANCE OF THE CAVE.

Soon Little Spider's web glittered silver and bright in the light of the moon on that cold, wintry night in the hills outside of Bethlehem.

Herod's soldiers stopped in front of the cave and Little Spider's frost-covered web.

Their footsteps no longer echoed in the coldness of the night.

Little Spider could hear their breathing, loud and harsh.

Pressed against the back wall inside the darkness of the cave, Man and Woman trembled. The Child slept in the Woman's arms.

Little Spider knew the soldiers had arrived to kill the Child that Man and Woman loved so dearly. The Child that angels had sung for on the night of his birth. The Child that angels had promised would bring peace to all the world.

Woman held the Child.

Man put his arms around Woman.

They closed their eyes in fear.

And waited for Herod's soldiers to burst into the cave.

nine

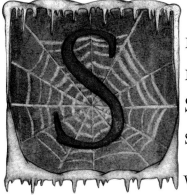 HALL WE SEARCH
INSIDE?" LITTLE
SPIDER HEARD A
SOLDIER ASK.

Woman bit her lip to keep
from crying out in fear.

Man drew even closer to Woman to protect her and
the Child with his body.

Little Spider peeked outside.

The moonlight clearly showed the Little Spider's web,
covered with silver frost, stretched across the entrance
of the cave.

"Let's not waste our time," the captain of Herod's

soldiers finally answered. "There is no one inside. Anyone entering would have torn that spider's web."

The soldiers passed on, leaving Man, Woman, and the Child in peace.

And the Child slept on.

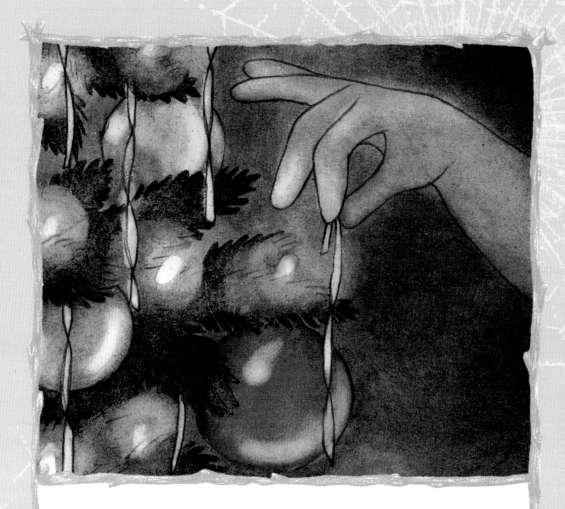

The story of the Little Spider is a retelling of an ancient legend. It is why, this lovely legend tells us, we put tinsel on our Christmas trees. The glittering streamers are a symbol of the Little Spider's web, beautiful with its frost, stretched across the entrance of the cave. Even though the story is based on legend, it truly reminds us that no gift given to Jesus, no matter how small, is ever forgotten.

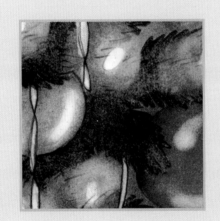

What Can I Give?

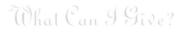

Cindy Morgan

Bundled there safe in the manger
heaven shines out from your eyes.
Halo around you
the angels surround you
and sing sweet lullabies.

So what in the world can I give you
that you don't already have?
Your Father in heaven
can hold all the stars
in the palm of his hand.

So tell me what can I give this Christmas?
What can I give?
What can I give?
What can I give?

You don't need rubies or diamonds,
frankincense, gold or myrrh.
But I have something
that no one else has
in the whole wide world.

So tell me what can I give this Christmas?
What can I give?
What can I give?
What can I give?

A time that the world will remember
far beyond when this moment is gone.
Oh to be with you.
I know what to give you
I know, I know.

I will give you my heart.
I will give you my heart.
I will give you my heart.

What can I give this Christmas?
What can I give?
What can I give?
What can I give?

I will give you my heart.

MyrG

11/01